D1402173

SCHOOLS ARE WHERE YOU FIND THEM

SCHOOLS ARE

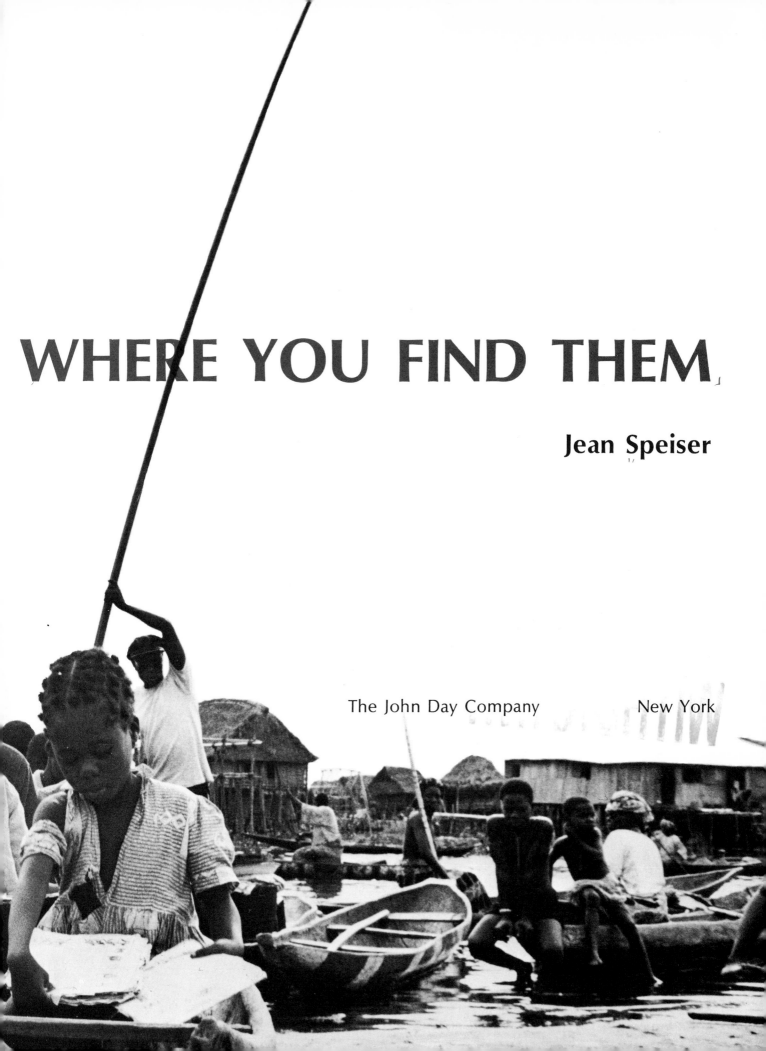

WHERE YOU FIND THEM

Jean Speiser

The John Day Company   New York

PICTURE CREDITS

Cover, John Balcomb

Balcomb, John, 15, 50
Bernheim, Marc & Evelyne, title page, 22, 37, 100, 101, 105
Carias, Fernando C., 33
Englebert, Victor, 80
Frank, Jerry, 46–7
Gerin, Bernard, 40, 58–9, 110–12
Grunzweig, B., 61, 114
Holton, George, 19, 53, 109
Kahler, Charlotte, 16
Kongsupto, P., 96–98
Kraus, Ilsa, 57, 91
Ling, Jack, 24, 30, 35, 41, 52, 60, 69, 72–3, 77, 86, 106–7
Massin, Alan, 26, 34
Matheson, Alastair, 65–8, 92–3
Mellett, Al, 18, 81, 108
Mielche, Haakon, 86
Miller, Ed, 56
Niclas, Yolla, 87
Norwegian Information Service, 78–9
Sennett, Tomas, 95
Shaw, Ray, 74
Spain, Clara, 71
Speiser, Jean, 17, 36, 48, 51, 116–8
UNICEF, 38–9, 54
UNESCO, Frontispiece, 31, 44–5, 49, 75, 88, 90, 94, 104
UNITED NATIONS, 20–1, 25, 55, 70, 89, 115
U.S. Information Service, 64
USSR, 76
Vajrathon, Mallica, 32

The John Day Company, 257 Park Avenue South, New York N.Y. 10010
An Intext Publisher

Published on the same day in Canada by Longman Canada Limited.

Library of Congress Catalogue Card Number: 70-135278
Printed in the United States of America

ages 7-10

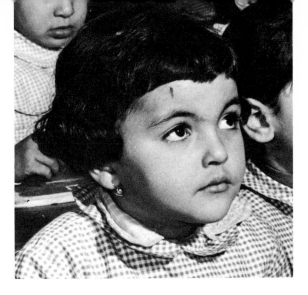

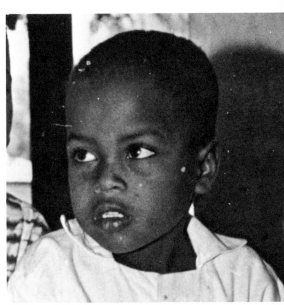

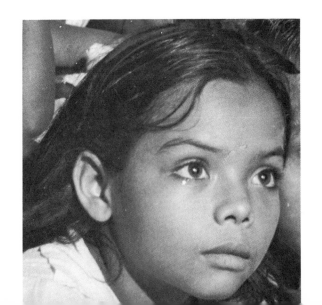

CONTENTS

FOREWORD

Most countries need help in educating their children. Because this is generally recognized and acknowledged, the United Nations made the right to learn a part of the Declaration of Human Rights in 1948, and reaffirmed it in 1959 with the Declaration of the Rights of the Child.

But "right" does not mean opportunity. So the efforts of two United Nations agencies have been directed specifically to education and to children, and to assisting governments in providing opportunities for children to learn. They are UNESCO (the Educational, Scientific and Cultural Organization), and UNICEF (the Children's Fund), who are at work in more than one hundred countries and among peoples of many cultures.

It is fitting that the United Nations, whose most compelling objective is world peace, should also be concerned directly with books and schools and teachers. For only when ignorance is no longer a way of life anywhere in the world will nations be able to live together in friendship and understanding.

ANDREW W. CORDIER

President, Columbia University

New York City

July 1970

SCHOOLS ARE WHERE YOU FIND THEM

Ten years ago, the United Nations made a list of good things they thought every boy and girl in the world should have from the day he was born. It was called The Declaration of the Rights of the Child.

One of these rights was *education*. This is what it said about it:

Every child should have free schooling.

He should be given a chance to develop his talents.

He should learn how to become a useful member of society.

He should be given a chance to play and enjoy recreation.

His parents and all the members of his community should help him to have these rights.

Every single country in the U.N. voted in favor of the Declaration. UNICEF, with other U.N. agencies, tried very hard to see that all children have a chance to read and write. It has done this by helping to train teachers and by sending books and blackboards and pencils, and desks and chairs and tables to schools that need them. It sends more help every year, but there are still many boys and girls all over the world who never go to school.

I

SCHOOLS ARE WHERE YOU FIND THEM

All over this world, there are boys and girls who do their lessons in classes held under a tree, or on a mountainside, or in a church.

Other children help to build their own schools. They carry rocks, or clay, or wood to make the walls. Then they make the stools they sit on and the tables they use for desks.

In many countries, schools are held in tents. In Canada there is a school in the car of a train. The engine hauls it back and forth between two areas every week. The students go to school on snowshoes or by sled, because the roads are covered with snow.

More than one hundred years ago, Abraham Lincoln went to school in a building made of logs, with a dirt floor and no heat except a tiny stove. Not too long ago, you might have been going to classes in a one-room schoolhouse.

On a mountaintop in Nepal (Neh-PAHL), at a height of 12,000 feet, children from a village hold classes on the ground. They carry their books and their lunches with them up the mountainside and say their lessons sitting in a circle. If you look closely maybe you can tell what time of day it is or whether it is hot or cold.

Timbuktu is a city in Mali (MA-lee), which is in Africa. It is on the very edge of the Sahara (Sa-HAIR-a) Desert. These schoolchildren live just outside the city and are learning to read from a book called the Koran (Kor-AN). It tells about the Moslem religion, one of the oldest in the world. They also study the history of their nation and copy letters on their wooden slates. The writing is Arabic (AIR-a-bic).

Maybe you are wondering about the shaved and half-shaved heads of some of the boys. Different families have different hair styles, just as some wear long hair and some wear short hair in other parts of the world.

In many schools, children help to raise their country's flag before school begins. That is what is happening here at one of the highest schools in the world, where the elevation (distance above sea level) is 15,000 feet. The flagpole tips a little, because it was made from a very tall tree.

The country is Bolivia (Bo-LIV-ee-a), at the very top of the Andes (AN-deez) Mountains in South America.

Just before sunset, the teachers help the pupils to lower the flag and put it away for the night.

Could you sit cross-legged for hours with just a mat between you and the floor? These boys do not seem to mind it. What sort of building do you think this is? There is one clue—the doorway on which the blackboard is leaning. It has many decorations of the sort found mostly in churches. The country is Afghanistan (Af-GAN-i-stan), a land of very high mountains.

What do you think the boys are learning?

A church mission house in Uganda (U-GAN-da) is the gathering place for this school whose classes are held in a field.

Can you find three girls here? They are very lucky to have a chance to go to school, and they walk long miles to get there.

Those students who come the farthest ride bicycles, for there are no buses and only a few automobiles in the rough country known as "the bush."

Can you tell what the mission house is built of? Why is it built that way?

A big straw mat marks the boundaries of this classroom. In this crowded school in Dacca, Pakistan (DAH-ka, PAK-i-stan), there are no walls between classrooms or doors. Yet everyone on this long mat knows he belongs to one class.

Those are first reading books we see. Why do you suppose the boy is pointing at that place on the page?

The big bronze bells hanging over these Guatemala (Guat-em-AH-la) children not only call them to school, but gather the people of the village together for church and for meetings. The girls are eating their free school lunch, with milk specially fortified to build strong teeth and bones. Their meals at home are largely corn and beans, and you know this would not give them all the nourishment they need. The girls dress like their mothers from the time they are very little, in brightly colored skirts and blouses woven in their own villages.

Learning your letters out of doors might be fun in nice weather. This country is Togo, and the sand and the palm trees tell you what the climate is like. These boys and girls come from families where the mother is at work all day long, or going to school herself. So the children spend all day at the school, and the teacher is like a second mother.

In Thailand (TIE-land) the heat often makes it uncomfortable to be inside, so, under a spreading tree, a third-grade class of boys recite for their teacher as she does arithmetic on a big blackboard. The girls, who are sitting across the aisle from the boys, will soon have their turn.

The big tree is called a banyan (BAN-yan). It is an unusual tree which sends roots down to the ground from its branches so that after a while its trunk becomes huge. In this very hot country it gives a welcome shade, as you can see by the bench which has been built around its base for resting.

In a tent with open sides, many children crouch on the ground because there are not enough benches. Half go to school in the morning, the others in the afternoon. Can you tell what they are doing when they hold up their fingers?

These children live in a camp for refugees (people who have left their homes because of war or disaster). Their former home was in Jordan.

This building that looks as though it were made of tree trunks is really built of mud which is baked hard by the sun. The poles are set in the mud crosswise before it dries to make the columns sturdy. The country is Upper Volta, in central Africa. The schoolhouse, which is one of the strangest you will find anywhere, is really a mosque (MOSK), a Moslem temple. Classes are not held every day but as often as possible. Would you like that?

There is a river near this primary schoolhouse in Guyana (Guy-AN-a) that floods during the rainy season. This should tell you why the school is built on stilts.

School meets from 8 to 11:30, and from 1 to 3 o'clock in the afternoon. The children look very happy, probably because they are on their way home.

II

GETTING THERE

Two thousand years ago, in Greece, there were no sidewalks or policemen as we know them, so parents sent along servants to keep the boy students from harm on their way to school. This special servant was called a "pedagogue" (PED-a-gog), which meant "one who leads on foot."

Many years later, when the Romans began their schools, it was the duty of these servants to coach groups of boys in their lessons as they walked along, so "pedagogue" grew to mean "teacher," as it does today.

On the island of St. Croix (SAINT CROY) in the Caribbean Sea, a young boy climbs aboard a passenger airplane each morning to attend school on a nearby island, St. Thomas. He returns on the same plane each afternoon at 5 o'clock. The trip takes twenty minutes, a shorter ride than most trips made by school buses.

In the Philippine Islands there is a school bus called a "jeepney." It stops at 7 a.m. and picks up seven children, all it can hold.

In Switzerland and in the far northern parts of Norway, Sweden, and Finland, many students ski downhill to school. But then they must climb the steep slopes at the close of the day.

In New York City, those children who do not walk to school use subways underground, public buses, or school buses.

In many suburban families the mother takes the father to the train station, then comes home to gather up her children and the children next door and take them to school.

But perhaps the most usual, and the pleasantest, way is to walk to school along a shady street or through the field or woods, with a friend.

Now let's see how many other ways there are of getting to school.

Feet get most children to school. After feet, school buses come next. This one might be anywhere, except for the words "Damodar (DAM-o-dar) Valley," which is named for a river in India. The corporation (*Corpn.*) builds power plants to produce electricity for the valley. Because most of the men moved their homes and families in order to work for the company, the company in return supplies schools and transportation for students.

These Togo children on their way to school carry little pillows on which they sit while reciting their lessons. They learn by memorizing what their teacher tells them or writes on the blackboard, so they do not have to carry books.

The girls carry the pillows on their heads, because that is the way their mothers have always carried their burdens. This teaches them to walk straight and tall, and hold their heads high. Could you carry your schoolbag home that way? Try it.

(Those large jars hold water, which may come from a long distance away.)

A motorboat large enough to carry a whole class and its teacher takes the children of Samud Songkramato (SA-mood-song-kra-MA-toe), Thailand, to school. The river Mae Klong is the village's main street, and people go everywhere by boat. This boat has canvas curtains rolled up now to the top deck, but during bad weather they are let down again. Thailand's rainy season lasts for several weeks.

In this picture the donkey, who is also called a burro, is the burden-bearer. He carries not only three brothers, but three cases full of books. They probably have a long way to go down the road you see in the distance. The country is Venezuela (Ven-ez-WAY-la), in the northern region of South America. The burro is as much of a family pet as dogs and cats are in North America.

A nomad child may have a long way to go, and camelback may be the only way to get there. Thus he learns to guide and control the camel as other children learn to ride horses. Do you know how this desert child, who looks very independent, will find his way down from the back of the camel?

The camel is almost too large to be called a pet, but he is a valuable member of an African desert family. These desert people are called "nomad," which means "wanderer," because they move their homes several times a year to find good pastures for their cattle, sheep, or goats. The camel is used to carry beds or rugs and even parts of houses on its back during these travel periods.

The country is Niger (NI-jer), which sounds very much like another country in Africa. Do you know what it is?

Some children walk beside the railroad tracks on their way to school; others walk on walls or along fences. The way to school in one part of Pakistan (PAK-i-stan) leads along a new water main (a giant pipe). This picture tells us two things about this country's progress. First, pure water is reaching people in rural regions and not only in the city. Second, girls are going to school, which was not true a few years ago. It is not likely that the mother of these girls had a chance to learn to read and write, but her daughters, as well as her sons, surely will.

The church is the center of every Latin-American village, as it is in this farm community in Peru (Pe-ROO). The road is rough and dusty, for it has been dug out of the same rocky soil that was used to make the graceful church towers in the distance. The little girls toiling up the hill from school live on small cotton farms three miles away. In rainy months, flood waters pour down from the big mountains nearby, causing the river in the valley to overflow. Then the children are not able to go to school for days and even weeks.

36

Here we see the mini-fleet of the water village of Ganvié (GAN-vee-ay) in the African Republic of Dahomey (Da-HO-may), which takes the children to school and their parents to market. The boats are called pirogues (pea-ROG). This is a French word that means a dugout canoe.

One school serves all the children who live in the houses on stilts. Their parents support the family by fishing. Some of them have lived all their lives on the water, but their children will go to high schools and college in the city.

The school bell has not yet rung, so primary-school students have time to go over their lessons before they leave the boats.

These boys are on their way to school on the island of Okinawa, near Japan. When the tide is too low for the school boat to carry them from their home island of Ou, the children use stilts to cross a channel of 1,500 feet. Is this more or less than a mile? Do you think it would be easier or harder to walk on stilts in the water? Why?

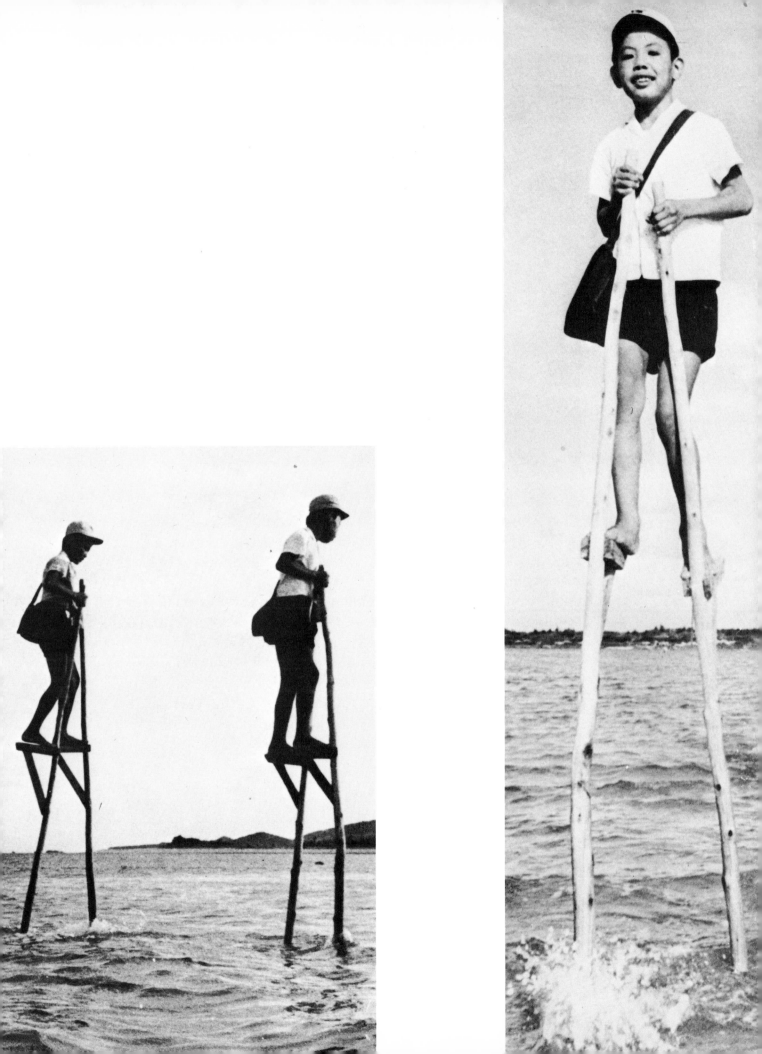

How would you like to have your school come to *you*? This is exactly what happens to children in Iran, a country in central Asia, who belong to tribes that live in the cool mountain areas in summer and go down to the warmer dry country in winter. As the families pack up and move, the school packs up and moves, too. It is called a "White Tent" school, to tell it apart from the black tents in which the people of the Fars tribe set up housekeeping. It is not difficult to move this school around, for all there is to it, besides a sturdy tent, are a blackboard, a folding chair for the teacher, a map of the world, and some books. The children bring along their own rugs to sit on because the ground is rocky and likely to be chilly.

What do they learn in this strange schoolhouse? Everything other children learn—reading, writing, arithmetic, social studies, singing and drama and sports. And the hours? 7:30 to 11:30 in the morning, and 2 to 6 p.m. Every school has 40 pupils, and there are 600 tent schools over the country. How many White Tent pupils does that make? Quite enough to make sure that children of wandering tribesmen will grow up with as good an education as children who have a street address and a mailbox.

In the white uniforms worn by all the children in Paraguay (PAR-a-goo-ay), a country in the very center of the South American continent, three small girls walk home under a cloudy sunset sky. When the clouds are rosy, the naturally red soil gives back the color and the lonely countryside seems to catch fire. These little girls live in a part of the country that has only lately been cleared of forest and jungle so that homes could be built. Their classmates come from many miles around. Like them, they are pioneers, helping to open a new future for their country by living in its rugged wilderness.

III

A NUMBER
IS A NUMBER

If you could fly backwards in time, you might land in ancient Greece. As a student in those days you would study the same subjects you are studying in school today—reading, writing, and arithmetic. Ever since those times, for two thousand years, life has been very hard for anyone who did not know how to read a book or write a letter or sign his name, or use money. You can probably think of many other things you would not be able to do if you did not know how to read or write.

Long ago, only boys of wealthy parents went to school. They did not study subjects that would help them to make a living. Then young men began to study law and medicine and, a long time later, girls were taught how to become teachers and nurses. Today, both boys and girls are given more chances to choose the kinds of lives they would like to lead. But in some countries people must still work very hard just to have homes and to stay in good health. They do not have many choices about their futures.

So, in those places, boys are taught very useful things, such as fishing and farming, and girls learn how to be good mothers and how to sew and cook. When times are better they will have more jobs for which to train and more schools in which to learn other things, such as science and world history and art.

But wherever they are in our world, students at school have a lot to learn. Much of what they study is the same everywhere. Sometimes, though, what a boy or girl studies is special to his country or his part of the world.

In the Republic of Korea, all children must go to school. One of the things they learn, too, is long division. Someone in this class seems to have had trouble. Can you find the mistake?

The picture at the right shows an outdoor art class.
The name of the school is Goonpo Primary School.

Guyana (Guy-AN-a) is one of the newest nations. Before it became independent it was called British Guiana. It has important seacoast cities, but it also has deep wilderness where Indians live in their own communities on land set aside by the government. The Indians want their children to learn English and other subjects taught in the city schools, so teachers are sent out to help them. Here is a class in arithmetic.

The story on the blackboard is a very good lesson in being
kind, as well as a lesson in writing. This is what it says.

STORY

One day an ant fell into a river.
He was drowning when a parrot saw him.
The kind bird picked a leaf and
dropped it in the river. The ant
climbed on the leaf and was saved.
He promised to do some kindness
for the parrot. Another day a
huntsman was about to shoot the
parrot. The ant saw. He quickly
ran up the huntsman's leg and bit him.
He fired his gun but he
missed the parrot. The ant
had saved the parrot's life.

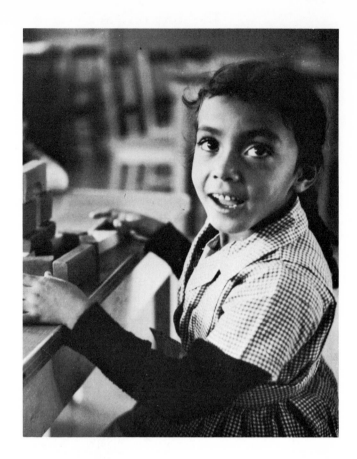

You may remember that you learned your colors from building blocks. They also taught you how to balance objects so they did not tumble, and how to use your hands carefully without dropping things.

These children, playing with blocks in the picture, go to a school in Honduras (Hon-DOO-rus), Central America, for children whose mothers work all day.

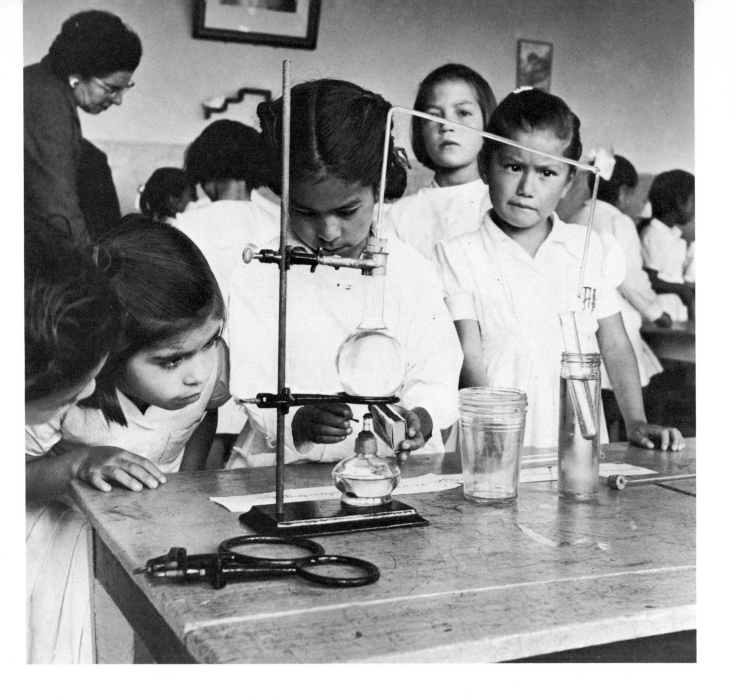

These children in an Ecuador (Eh-kwa-DOOR) primary school are finding out how rain is formed. They are thinking for themselves, rather than learning everything from a book. Could you explain it to them if you were with them?

In Nepal, science is taught in the very early grades. You may have played the game shown here: "What is in the box?" The children try to find out by shaking the box and listening to the sound it makes, and feeling how heavy it is.

The best pupil in the class built a little lab at home. Can you tell what experiment he is doing here with this glass and piece of cardboard?

In Guatemala, women and girls make pottery. This is a very old art. The dishes are made of clay, and are shaped into saucers and bowls and cups while the clay is still wet. Then it is baked in the sun, or in an oven, and often given a shiny finish called "glaze," or painted. Skilled potters can sell their wares for money or exchange them for food.

The girls of Chinutla (Chin-OOT-la) learn this in their school, which has just four grades. There are not enough teachers in this country to take care of the children who want to go to school. The government is trying out a new kind of school that goes to the sixth grade. It has only one teacher, but she knows how to teach every grade!

In Burma, children learn about hygiene in school health clubs. The older children are officers, and inspect the younger ones regularly. In the picture above, teeth are being examined.

This child (below) will get a mark against her record because her nails are not neatly trimmed. What other things besides hair and teeth and nails are important if you are to look neat and clean?

Schoolboys in Kenya (KEN-ya) have exercise classes each morning, to build muscles in every part of their bodies. It is not easy to hold this position without falling over. Try it. What part of the body is made stronger?

Just about the only way to learn to sew is by doing it. This class of girls in Venezuela is learning to sew without a machine, making fine tablecloths, embroidered pillowcases, and other things for their homes. The school has a pretty name: Teresa de Tuy (Te-RAY-se day TWEE).

Does this library in India remind you of yours? How is it different?

Does the sign tell you anything about the language of the country? In many places, children learn to speak two or three languages in the lower grades. These children know both English and their own dialect.

In North America, boys play football. In Central and South America, all the boys, big and little, play soccer. It is very much like football. There are eleven players on each team, and they try to get the ball (which is round, like a basketball) to the goal line before the other side takes it. There is one rule that makes this game very special: the players are not permitted to touch the ball with their hands. They may kick it or bounce it off their heads and shoulders, but they must never throw it. Would you think this game is more difficult than football?

The country is Panama (Pan-a-MA). What else do you know about this country?

You would not know it, but these boys and girls can neither hear nor speak. They attend a special school for such children in Colombia (Co-LOM-bee-ah). Their handicap makes it very much harder for the teacher to teach them, but she has many ways of helping them, for she is specially trained to do this. One picture on the wall shows speaking by means of hand signs. Next to it is a calendar. The month is "Marzo." What does that sound most like in English?

At the Al Harobe primary school outside a large city in Egypt, boys learn to do very useful things in a vocational class. ("Vocation" means "work.") They find out how to use metal, how to operate woodworking machines, and the proper way to use hand tools. This gives them a choice of many trades to follow when they have finished school. The boy here is making a birdcage. Soon he will be turning out larger pieces, such as lamps and bookcases.

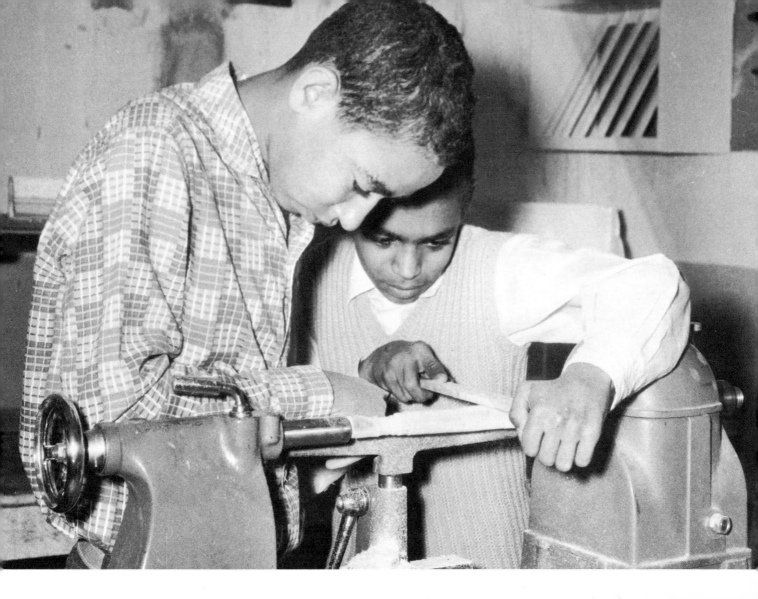

The boys above are working on a lathe, which gives a rounded surface to wood. Below, another student learns to use a hammer and chisel to split wood and metal and stone.

Using one of the tools his teacher has given him, this boy is working hard to break up the dry soil and give the roots of these fine cabbages a chance to spread and grow. Do you know whether you have to plant new cabbage seeds each year, or whether they will grow from last year's roots?

The garden is on the grounds of a school in Ecuador and the children are in charge of it.

Do you have a school garden, too?

Maybe the stop sign that helps you to cross the street looks
a little different from this one.

Perhaps your crossing guard is a parent or a traffic officer.
Here, in Jerusalem, it is an older student.

What do you think the broad, white lines on the street mean?

IV

THERE ARE MANY WAYS TO LEARN

Have you ever gone to the beach and made words or pictures on the sand with a stick or a shell?

This is how people first began to teach one another, at the desert or the seashore. For a long time there were no school buildings even after reading and spelling were known.

The Greeks and Romans sat on steps or on the seats of their stadium (STA-dee-um: a big playground), which were carved out of stone. When they did begin to write, they used a sharp stick called a stylus (STY-lus) on a kind of slate covered with wax. The words were rubbed off when they had finished the page. Another early forerunner of paper was papyrus (pa-PIE-rus), flattened sheets made from the pulp of the papyrus tree, first grown in Egypt. Boys carried a rolled sheet to school in a long wooden box.

After that came slates and blackboards and, finally, when printing was invented, we had books!

A giant map of the United States is laid out in chalk on the
grounds of this school in Colorado. The children hop from
state to state, to see how many they can touch without step-
ping on a line. Each of the states in the U.S. mainland has
several touching neighbor states. Can you think of two states
that have no neighbor states touching theirs?

The island country of Mauritius (Mor-ISH-us) is out in the Indian Ocean far away from land. It is difficult for these students to think of a country that is not surrounded by water.

This giant map in their schoolyard shows them the shape of the island. The hills and highlands are molded in the clay to rise a bit above the ocean. This kind of map with ridges for mountains and flat areas for deserts is called a relief map.

Learning to count can be fun when you use fingers and toes. In a primary school in Nigeria (Ni-JEER-ee-ah), it is this little girl's turn to have the sole of her foot painted by another student. Next, she will step on a long sheet of paper to leave her footprint.

First, the children count feet. Then, after they have learned the lower numbers, they count everyone's toes. Before many days have passed, everybody can count and add or subtract toes!

What do you use in your classroom—checkers, marbles, milk cartons, crayons?

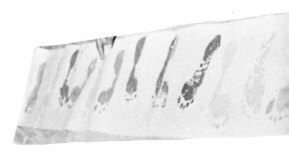

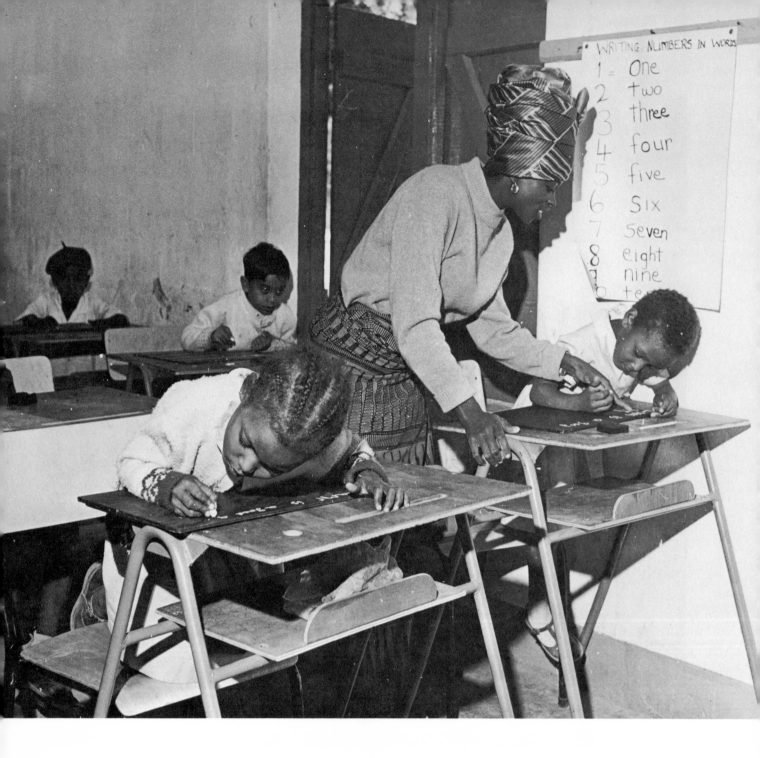

Another class in Nigeria is learning to *spell* numbers, which is a new idea to them. Each one is trying to write a sentence using a number from one to ten.

Their beautiful teacher wears a hat called a turban, and a skirt worn by all the women in her country, which is made up of many gay colors.

In countries where teachers cannot be trained fast enough to keep up with the need, older students often teach younger ones.

This is what happens in parts of Pakistan, where there are not enough schools in some places, and where many more teachers are very much needed.

How do you think this class in Nicaragua (Nik-a-RA-goo-a) is being taught? What makes you think so?

The subject is health, and the children are learning about flies and mosquitoes and other insects that spread disease. This is very useful to them, for in hot countries like theirs, there are many more harmful insects than in cold countries.

Nicaragua is one of the countries of Central America.

How to make words out of letters is a game which is played in primary schools in Algiers. This city is the capital of the country of Algeria (AL-JEER-ee-ah), in North Africa. Algerian children make their words in French, for that is the official language of the country. Perhaps you can think of some words that are the same in English and in French. *Café* is one; *crèche* is another, and there are many more.

This school traffic sign in Algeria would say in English "Right of way to the children." Can you name the languages in which it is written? What do your school street signs say?

الاولوية للاطفال
PRIORITÉ AUX ENFANTS

The "bamboo hop" is not as easy as it may look. It is a little bit like jumping rope, but instead of a rope, two bamboo poles are clapped together, and the children jump in and out. If someone catches a foot between the poles, his turn is over. This is a favorite way to spend recess at schools in China (Taiwan). The big long building on the hill is North Leaf School.

Is your playground on the roof of the school? This one is, because space is very precious in the city–state of Hong Kong, which is an island. It's also a great trade center, and ships and airplanes carry many goods between Asia and North America across the Pacific Ocean.

This is an exercise class. What do you think the teacher has just asked the students to do?

73

There's no escape anywhere in the world from drilling multiplication tables! Slates are still more used than books in most parts of the world. They are really very sensible, for you can easily rub out a wrong number. The children in these pictures did not do that, however. These schoolrooms are in Fez, a city in Morocco (Mor-RAH-ko), which is the center of art and music and writing.

One way of learning history is by celebrating the holidays your country keeps, and by doing the same things that have been done on that day for hundreds of years.

In Japan, the Boys' Festival is held every May 5. The children make paper hats and jackets and gay banners. This banner is made to look like a carp, a fish that is much admired in Asian countries for its strength and courage. Of course, there is a Girls' Day, too. It is a Festival of Dolls, called Hinamatsuri (HIN-a-mat-SOO-ree). It is held every year on March 3.

75

In Moscow, the capital of Russia, these students have just received their books on their first day at school. Schools open on the same day—September 1—all over Russia. It is a day of national celebration, in which the students take flowers to give to their teachers.

Russian schools are rather strict. Report cards are issued every week, and students are checked every day for their neatness of dress, good manners, and their speech. Each child also has daily schoolroom tasks to perform.

A boy who wishes to be a scientist must take biology (the study of plants and animals) in the fourth grade, foreign languages in the fifth grade, and chemistry in the seventh grade. After he passes the tenth grade, he takes a state examination, which sometimes lasts a whole month. In addition to book studies, girls can take not only sewing and cooking, but carpentry and metalworking.

Children who have special talents attend schools in ballet, music, or art, and often study sixteen hours a day.

One way of learning is by handling objects and fitting large and small sizes and shapes into their proper places. These girls are in a nursery school in Bombay, India. Do you remember when you first did this? It was probably before you knew how to spell or read.

These kindergarten pupils in Norway are on a field trip. Their lunches are in their schoolbags. Why do you suppose they carry them strapped to their backs?

What are some of the things you could learn on a winter field trip?

Almost every schoolchild in Norway knows how to ski and skate. These children have won diplomas in a skiing contest. This is like winning a blue ribbon in a track meet.

Niger, in the very center of Africa, has the simplest kind of schools for the nomad children who live in the desert. (Do you remember the boy on the camel?) But children who live in the capital city of Niamey (NI-a-may) in Niger learn by the most modern television programs.

These boys and girls who are now in the third grade have been learning their lessons from TV programs ever since they started school. They are waiting to see a program telling how families live in France.

The government believes this is the best way of teaching its children and hopes it can keep on doing this. It is more expensive than holding classes without television. Would you like to learn this way?

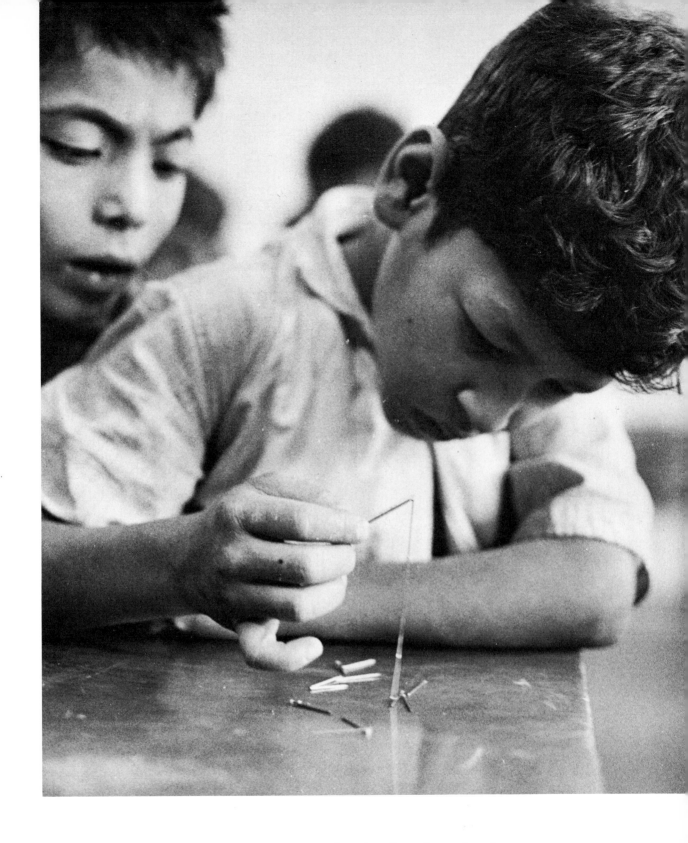

A little boy in Nepal is discovering for the first time that he can pick up small nails with a piece of steel called a magnet. Have you ever tried this? Can you explain why it happens?

This is another way to teach a child who cannot see. Small models of familiar things, such as automobiles, spoons, cups and fishes are strung across a frame. As the lad feels them, he learns their names, and then he will remember what they are like when he touches the real objects. This child goes to school in the Philippine Islands, where blind children are enrolled in public school, as they are in Ceylon. *Touch* is one of the five senses everyone has. Do you know what the others are?

V

WHAT BELONGS IN A SCHOOL?

As we have just seen in the pages we've read, there are a great many ways to learn. Books and good school buildings and machines help. But other things are needed, too. From this list, see if you can select five things you could not possibly do without:

Blackboards	Baseballs
Cafeterias	Slide projectors
Notebooks	Typewriters
Gymnasiums	Chalk
Desks	Crayons
Something to sit on	Film projectors
Windows	Sports equipment
Pencils	Toilets
Television	Drinking fountains
Record players	Wash basins
Books	Paper
Playgrounds	Erasers
Report cards	

Now make another list of things you would like to have in your school that you do not have. Would you exchange any of them for those in your first list?

It may seem odd to you, but children in Burma are used to doing their lessons without desks or tables. As we have noted, the very first schools were held in the same way, without classrooms or furniture. In the upper grades students sat on benches that were *higher* than those used by the younger children. This is how "high schools" got their name.

Below, what game might the children be playing?

A Japanese child's copybook contains page after page of pictures as well as notes, drawn and colored by the students themselves. There are fifty-one symbols in the Japanese alphabet. Before they master them, the children learn words from stories and poems. This little girl's carefully written story is in English. In a number of countries where English is not the language of the land, children begin to study it just the same in the first grade.

Records are used to teach music and languages. These children are being helped by them in a school in Peru near Lima (LEE-ma), a large city on the seacoast. Photographs, drawings and radios and TV are other kinds of teaching tools. Children in hospitals or children who are sick at home keep up in their lessons with help from them.

This is not a real mosquito. If it were, it would make a person very ill indeed. It is a large model of a dangerous insect in India that carries a disease known as malaria (ma-LAIR-ee-a). When it bites, it leaves an infection that gets into the blood and causes a very high fever. It brings on chills in the hottest weather, and often death. Children suffer from it more than older persons. So they are told about the illness in school, and about how they can best keep from having it. This giant mosquito travels from school to school in its big box, teaching as it goes. It is sent from a government health center in a large city.

Climbing poles are the best-liked part of this gymnasium in Geneva, Switzerland. They help to build strong arms and legs, and it is fun to see if you can get all the way to the top. Do you have anything like them in your gym?

In Switzerland, where the most famous mountains in the world—the Alps—are found, everyone goes skiing. Children do not attend school on Thursday afternoons, which are kept for school holidays. This often means a skiing trip. To make up the time, classes are held on Saturday mornings.

Here is a Greek boy who had polio. He has to work hard to learn to use his hands and to walk again. The big blocks are easier for him to handle in playing dominoes than the little ones, which slip from his fingers. Drawing and painting help, too. He could not move his right hand when he first began to help himself, but at the end of six months, he could use a knife and fork, tie his shoelaces, and dress himself.

He goes to a school for handicapped children, where he is given many kinds of treatment to build his muscles and help his hands and feet work together again. Driving a mini-automobile helps and it's fun!

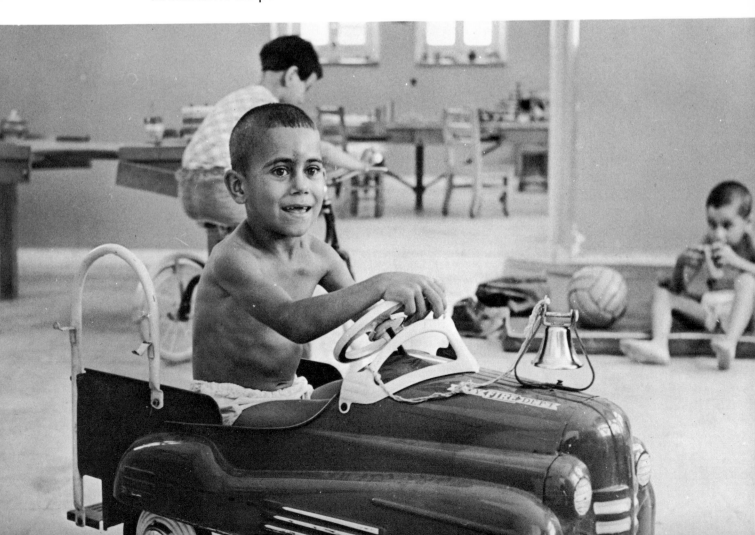

In Somalia, an African desert land, the nomad children go to school under a thorn tree. The hot sun finds its way through the spindly branches, and the dust whirls when the wind blows. Subjects are reading, writing (in Arabic), and figures.

Here you can see the slates, which are made of wood. Pens are sharp sticks, and the ink is made from the juices of plants. The teacher is correcting the writing on the soft wood of the slate. Arabic is written from right to left.

The townspeople of Upper Volta build their own schools, like this one made of bricks. The desks are shaped from clay, instead of from wood. Can you think why?

Upper Volta is an African country that takes its name from two rivers—the Black Volta and the White Volta. They help to water the farmland, for the country is very dry. Now do you know why the desks are not made of wood?

Almost all the men are farmers, and the boys and girls who go to school learn about gardening along with other subjects. They often go home and show their parents better ways to take care of their farms.

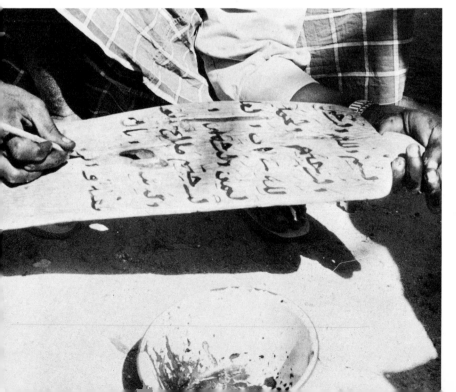

Here you can see the slates, which are made of wood. Pens are sharp sticks, and the ink is made from the juices of plants. The teacher is correcting the writing on the soft wood of the slate. Arabic is written from right to left.

The townspeople of Upper Volta build their own schools, like this one made of bricks. The desks are shaped from clay, instead of from wood. Can you think why?

Upper Volta is an African country that takes its name from two rivers—the Black Volta and the White Volta. They help to water the farmland, for the country is very dry. Now do you know why the desks are not made of wood?

Almost all the men are farmers, and the boys and girls who go to school learn about gardening along with other subjects. They often go home and show their parents better ways to take care of their farms.

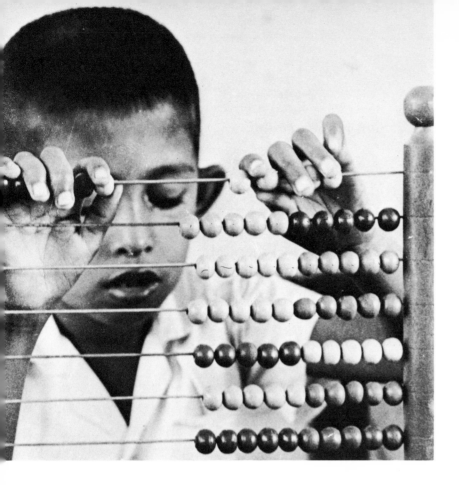

This child lives on the island of Ceylon (See-LON), near India, and he is blind. He is using an abacus, a very old teaching tool invented by the Greeks and Romans thousands of years ago. By moving the wooden balls across the string, he can learn to count and do arithmetic. What is he adding here?

Ceylon is one of the first countries to teach blind children in the same school with children who can see. The boy's teacher gives him a great deal of help, and his classmates watch over him on the playground. He is doing so well that he will be able to keep up with his grade and perhaps go to college.

Fishnets are standard equipment in this school.

The palm trees tell us this country must be in a very warm place. It is. Its name is Thailand, and it is in the South Pacific. Just outside the capital city, Bangkok, there is a school where boys are taught not only to study books, but also to work with their hands. These boys are learning to mend the nets. Fishing is one of the world's biggest industries, so they should have no trouble finding work when they no longer go to school.

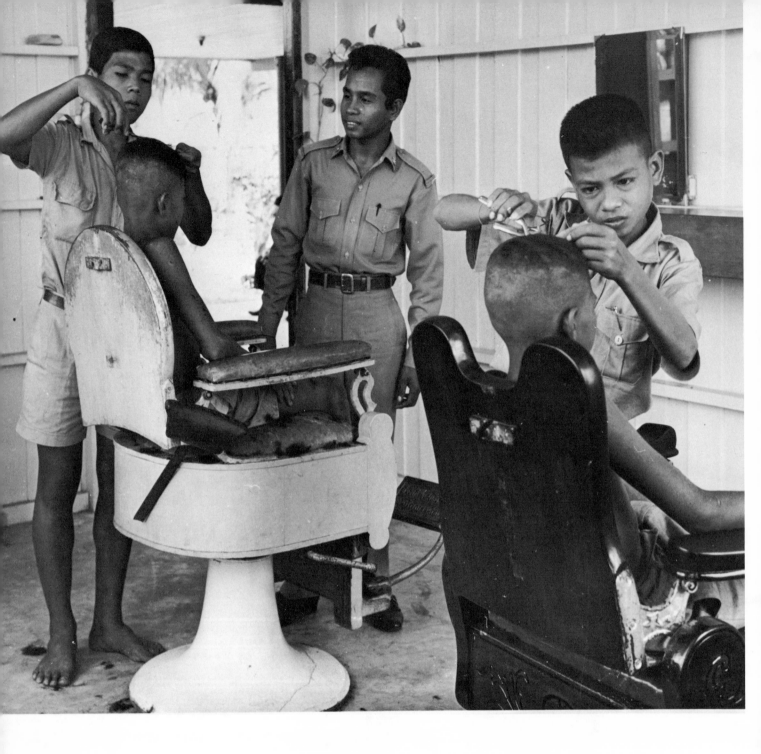

This looks like a very strange classroom, but the barber chairs are indeed part of the school's equipment. These boys are learning to cut their classmates' hair so that they will have a trade to help them earn a living. Others, like the boys in the previous picture, learn skills that their country will always need. Still others study woodworking, metalworking, and how to repair machinery. Do you think you would like this kind of instruction before you finish school?

A kibbutz (KI-Boots) is a type of big farm in Israel where many families live in a community and share everything.

At this kibbutz school where these children live, each boy and girl has his own little closet with his name on it, for toothbrush and towel. And here you see the boys' laundry hanging up to dry.

Children in a kibbutz have a great deal of fun because they have many playmates all the time.

What would you like about a kibbutz?

What would you miss?

In the Fiji Islands, which are located in the South Pacific, there are no school bells. Instead, hollow logs make a kind of drum for the children to beat when it is time for school to begin. This makes a loud sound that can be heard by anyone within sight of the schoolhouse. Boys take turns getting to school early so that they can beat on the log.

Jonamoukro primary school in the Ivory Coast (of Africa) was built by the village residents. They also made the benches the children carry on their heads to school each morning. The heavy roof, which is made of palm leaves, keeps out the sun and the rain and helps to make a very snug schoolhouse. In the same place, classes are held at night for the mothers and fathers of the children. Many of them have never been to school before now.

VI

TEACHERS ARE SPECIAL

If you learn to know and like your teachers, you will probably learn a great deal more easily. Most teachers know this, and try very hard not only to find the best ways of teaching but also to know their pupils so that they can make them happy while they are learning. They also try to help the students who have trouble with certain subjects, or have special problems.

Most teachers go to school themselves so that they can do a better job. These are the fortunate ones. In countries where teachers are needed very badly, they do not have time to go to school for very long. They start to teach as soon as they themselves have learned to read and write.

Most teachers are eager to share with their students what they have learned. They want to give away what they know, and not keep it for themselves. If you like to show your younger brothers and sisters how to read, or how to skate or swim, you might be a very good teacher. This is something to think about while you are learning.

Paraguay schools sometimes have several grades taught by the same teacher. This one has four grades, with seventy students who are six to ten years old. This keeps her very busy, but she has time to help the youngest pupil, who is just learning to print. She guides his hand across the page by taking it in hers, so he can feel her fingers move as they print.

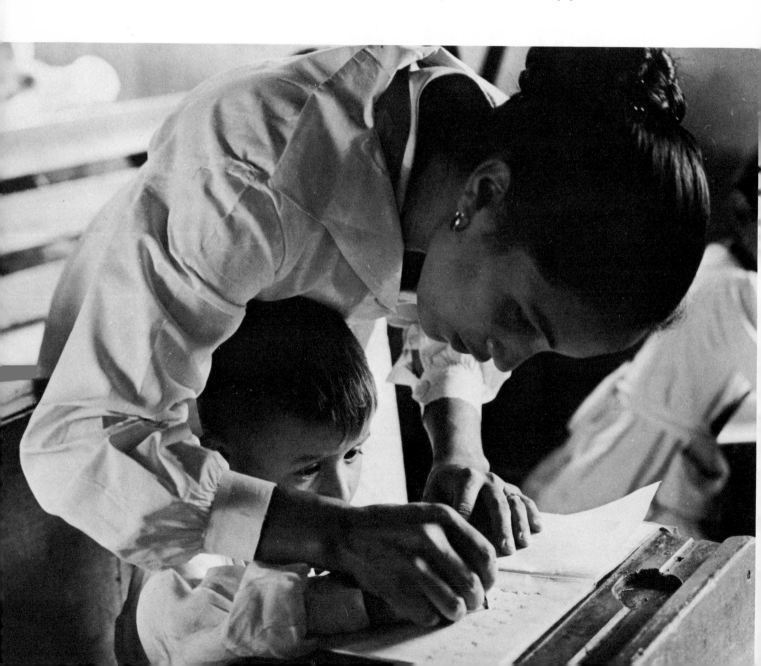

This teacher is only seventeen years old. She is still going to school, and teaches when she is not going to class herself. She is studying to be a social worker. Her name is Aminatou (Am-in-AH-too), and she likes to be with children. She has younger brothers and sisters of her own and plays with them a great deal. The children are learning a song in French. This is the language of their country, which is Cameroun. In her spare time she is learning how to type while one of her brothers watches with great interest.

105

A teacher in Rinconada, Ecuador, has many classes with both boys and girls. One of the girls' classes is sewing, and here she shows them how to use a machine. The material is woven in the village by mothers and grandmothers, and the children will be able to have more dresses and suits because sewing goes so much faster with a machine. These little girls are waiting to try it out.

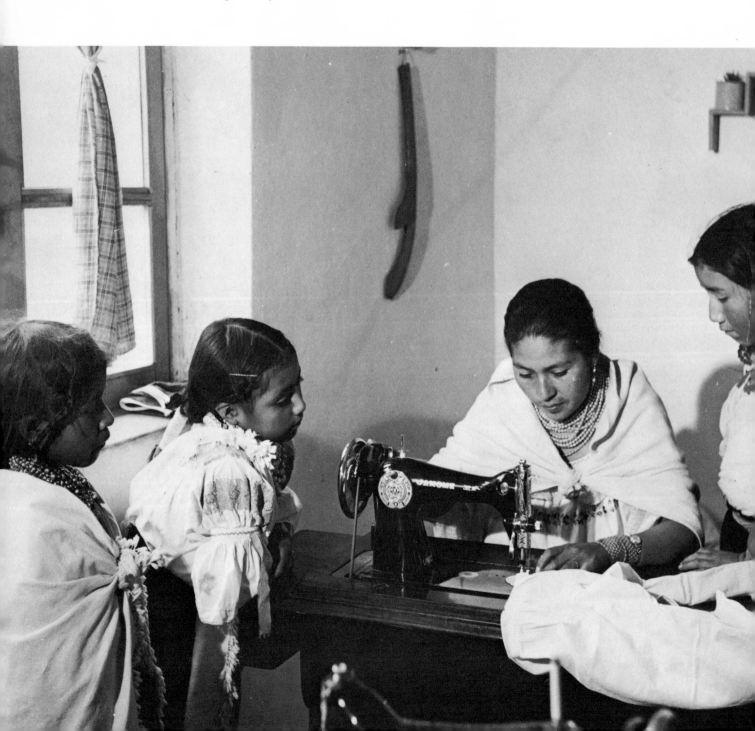

This same teacher is showing the boys which tools they will need for the school garden. It is not easy to grow vegetables in the mountains where this school is located, for the soil is hard and rocky, and there is not much rain. Rinconada is in a valley amid the peaks of the Andes Mountains 10,000 feet above sea level.

This is the Afghanistan schoolroom we saw on page 18, but this picture gives us a better look at the teacher. He seems very proud of his pupil's neat numbers. Writing in Arabic is from right to left. This child is writing 3000. Each dot means "zero." Can you find the 3?

Do you think writing in Arabic is easier or harder than writing in English?

Kindergarteners in Cairo (KY-ro), Egypt, learn to write by copying their letters from the blackboard. This teacher stops at each desk to see how well the children are doing and whether they understand.

Here is a teacher who plays games with his students as well as teaching school. In Iran, where the children go to school in tents, the teacher becomes a part of the family. He comes out to the mountains from the city and sleeps in the tent and eats there when classes are not being held. So he is much more than a teacher. He is also a close neighbor and a good friend.

Here he makes up his bed for the night after classes have ended for the day. He often takes supper with his pupils' parents.

Children live and go to school in their own little village on this kibbutz in Israel. They see their parents every day, but they study and eat and sleep in their schools.

This makes teachers very important, for they are like adopted parents as well. You see them here, eating with the children, and resting on the steps after playing in the garden.

A very little pupil is learning to write, and he gets help from a kindly teacher. These children spend a great deal of time in school because their parents are very busy building homes in a part of Japan where no one has lived before. It is called the Ishikari River valley. For many years it was covered with the ashes of nearby volcanoes.

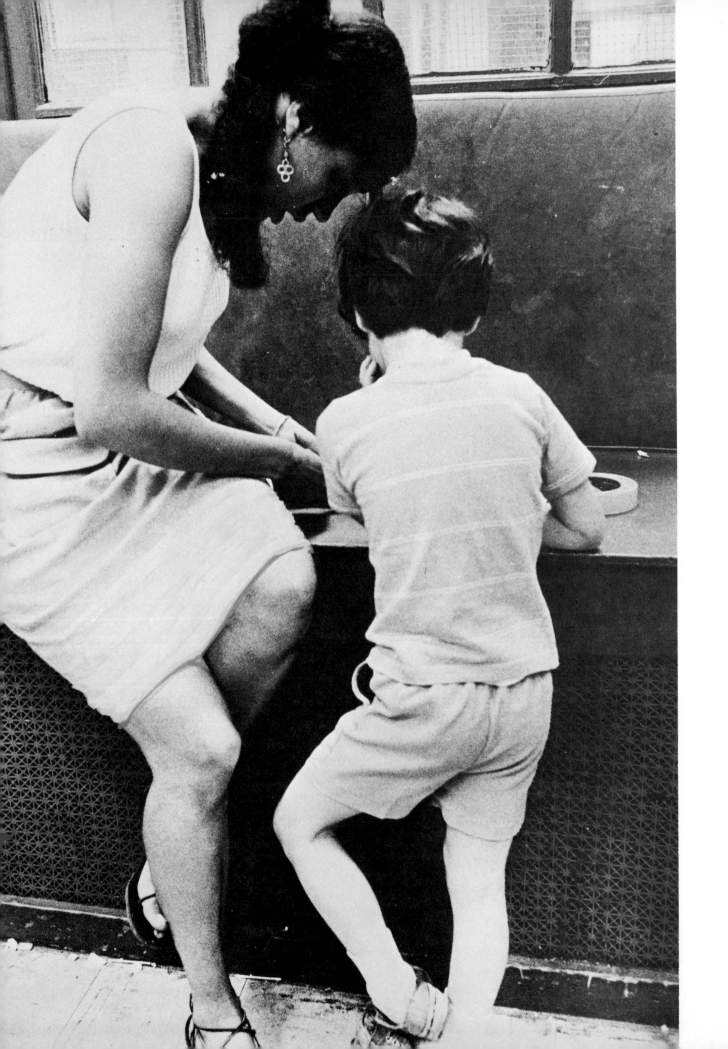

The Manhattan Country School in New York has classes in the city and in the country as well.

There are no desks. The children do their work wherever it seems right, at a table or a bench or on the floor, and the teachers are always available to help them, like the teachers we see here.

117

The grades are called by the children's ages. First grade is known as "Sixes," because all the children are six years old. They learn not only how to read and write, but also how to make things with their hands.

So you see there are as many ways of learning as there are cultures.

Under a tree, on top of a mountain, or in a tent, you hear the droning of the alphabet or the multiplication table, or their equivalents.

It does not matter how or where you learn. What matters is the result.

The boy who races to a thatched-roof schoolhouse carrying his "desk" on his head may return to his village some years later wearing a physician's white coat and carrying a black satchel full of things to heal his sick.

The small girl in the Pakistan hill country who sits on the ground wrapped in a handwoven shawl while she learns her letters could, with reason, exchange that shawl within a decade for the snappy uniform of an airlines hostess.

What will you be doing in ten years?

INDEX

About the Author

Jean Speiser has reported on children and learning in many places, both in words and pictures, for LIFE Magazine, the United States Information Service, and the United Nations, where she is picture editor of UNICEF.

She has felt very strongly that there is too much emphasis placed on the physical plant and equipment of schools, and that the eagerness of the pupil and the patience and generosity of the teachers are far more important components in the learning process.

These convictions were strengthened when, as a picture editor at the United Nations, she began to assemble photographs of schools and pupils and teachers from different parts of the world. It became even more evident to her that from the simplest and most rugged conditions of learning, useful adults might emerge in great numbers, and that the child to whom learning came hard might, in the end, make the most valuable contribution.